Managing ADHD a[nd Anxiety in] Teens 1[01]:

Simple Techniques to E[ffectively Manage] ADHD, Anxiety, and Stress for Teens

By

Sarah Fisher

Goldfish Books

© **Copyright 2022 by (Goldfish Books Sub Brand of Storesum Inc) - All rights reserved.**

Without the prior written permission of the Publisher, no part of this publication may be stored in a retrieval system, replicated, or transferred in any form or medium, digital, scanning, recording, printing, mechanical, or otherwise, except as permitted under 1976 United States Copyright Act, section 107 or 108. Permission concerns should be directed to the publisher's permission department.

Legal Notice

This book is copyright protected. It is only to be used for personal purposes. Without the author's or publisher's permission, you cannot paraphrase, quote, copy, distribute, sell, or change any part of the information in this book.

Disclaimer Notice

This book is written and published independently. Please keep in mind that the material in this publication is solely for educational and entertaining purposes. All efforts have provided authentic, up-to-date, trustworthy, and comprehensive information. There are no express or implied assurances. The purpose of this book's material is to assist readers in having a better understanding of the subject matter. The activities, information, and exercises are provided solely for self-help information. This book is not intended to replace expert psychologists, legal, financial, or other guidance. If you require counseling, please get in touch with a qualified professional.

By reading this text, the reader accepts that the author will not be held liable for any damages, indirectly or directly, experienced due to the information included herein, particularly, but not limited to, omissions, errors, or inaccuracies. You are accountable for your decisions, actions, and consequences as a reader.

About the Author

Sarah Fisher is a Child and Behavioral Therapist. She has a deep understanding of daily life problems like anxiety, depression, trauma, and other such types. She is keen to share all the knowledge with reasons, problems, and solutions so that the readers are successful in keeping such issues to a minimum. She is fully aware of the modern-day therapies that are helpful in tackling issues like anxiety and childhood trauma. She addresses personality and social disorders that can affect our lives in one way or another. She is keen to help the readers in the best possible manner by exploring the issues deeply and then coming up with the best possible solutions. Sarah wants the readers not to worry anymore if their kids are suffering from issues like childhood trauma or other anxiety disorders, as her books are a complete package when it comes to the perfect handling of such issues using modern tips and techniques.

Table of contents

INTRODUCTION 5

CHAPTER 1: ADHD BRAIN WIRING 10

1.1 Psychology of ADHD 11

1.2 Living and Thriving with ADHD 18

CHAPTER 2: FOCUS AND IMPULSIVENESS TOOLKIT 26

2.1 When My Focus is Out of Whack 27

2.2 Where is the Foresight? 35

CHAPTER 3: ORGANIZATION AND DISCIPLINE TOOLKIT 43

3.1 Enough with the Mess 43

3.2 Solider on the Front 51

CHAPTER 4: STRESS AND ANXIETY TOOLKIT 59

4.1 Hold the Stress 60

4.2 Ease Up the Anxiety 65

CONCLUSION 75

Introduction

A meta-analysis of 175 papers on the prevalence of ADHD in children aged 18 and under-produced a pooled estimate of 7.2 percent.

This percentage makes up 129 million children around the globe.

You are not alone in this. Take a deep breath.

A teenager like you shares his experience with ADHD:

"There are no windows, so my eyes are drawn to my classroom's orange door. My foot bounces up and down during the presentation, and my attention pings about. My lecturer is only a few steps away, but he fades in and out of my peripheral vision.

I switch back and forth between the PowerPoint presentation on the screen and the notes on my computer. I haphazardly enter bullet points. A ripple of laughter occasionally waves through the classroom. The questions and stories of my classmates and my professor's comments whirl around me and fill the room.

This is not a dull class. This lecture about mental health and exercise piques my interest. My professor does his hardest to keep us entertained by telling us hilarious and entertaining anecdotes.

My attention is still bouncing from one thing to another like a pinball. Even though I want to focus and am working hard to do so, the lecture is the last thing on my mind. But I'm distracted by the cacophony of sounds coming from my classmates — coughs, pens, zippers, keyboard clicks...

Soon after, I discovered that I was suffering from attention deficit hyperactivity disorder (ADHD), the diagnosis transformed my life. After years of feeling strange and struggling in silence, the most significant benefit was developing a greater understanding of myself — and why I see the world the way I do.

ADHD does not define me. It only helps me better understand who I am."

ADHD stands for Attention Deficit Hyperactivity Disorder. It is a mental health condition causing excessive hyperactivity and impulsivity. People who have ADHD may also struggle with remaining still for longer periods or focusing on a single task.

Many people endure energy fluctuations and inattention. It happens more frequently and to a greater extent in people battling with ADHD than those who do not have the disorder. It can have an enormous impact on their studies, work, and personal lives.

If you are a teenager nowadays, trying to fit in — or trying not to be noticed if you do not fit in — puts a lot of mental pressure.

Teens go to great lengths to avoid influencing unwanted attention, and when you have to manage the effects of ADHD, hiding away is not an option. Most teenagers lack the courage and maturity to accept and understand their differences. Explaining it to their friend is a whole another thing.

ADHD, a neurodevelopmental condition is associated with poor executive function. Executive abilities are required to manage emotions, behave autonomously, identify the need for aid, set and attain goals, and start almost anything,

The amount of effort required to go through a school day may make you feel frustrated, nervous, and entirely overwhelmed. Ordinary things like being organized, engaging in a conversation, keeping on track, and finishing homework projects (assuming you remembered to note them down right and have the materials needed to complete the tasks) become huge problems when executive functioning is impaired.

I have not even mentioned peer pressure, pimples or, periods, let alone negotiating other teen milestones such as learning to drive, using alcohol/ drugs, or engaging in sex! Things can get serious when you combine all of this with ADHD impulsivity.

Academic and social expectations rise during high school. At school and at home, teens have less structure and more autonomy, and teachers have less control when it comes to submitting assignments and keeping up with course. For ADHD teens, your newly found independence can backfire, exacerbating some of your symptoms.

Okay, so how can I help you manage ADHD?

I have developed this book focusing on the key areas an ADHD teenager struggles to keep up with in life. This book is divided into two parts. The first part deals with helping you understand ADHD, your brain psychology, and how it shows up in your life. It will also bust some myths about ADHD as the subject is quite confused about what it is not. It will also point out the perks of ADHD, so you know how to use it to your advantage. This part aims to help you understand yourself the best before we start discussing solutions.

The second part of the book deals with the major issues of ADHD life like impulsiveness, maintaining focus, staying organized and disciplined, and keeping your stress and anxiety in check. This part will offer practical strategies for you to apply in these challenging aspects.

Why should you believe anything I say?

I am a behavioral therapist dealing especially with ADHD and anxiety clients with an extensive experience of 7 years. Most of my clients are teenagers giving me insight into hundreds of versions of how a teenager behaves likes with ADHD and what to do about it. Whatever issues you are feeling overwhelmed with right now, chances are I have already dealt with them successfully. I am eager to help you in this journey, just like my own daughter. She was diagnosed with ADHD very early in age, and parenting her has given me an even more in-depth overview of the subject. The strategies mentioned in the book are what I try to include in my daughter's routine, and I have seen an incredible difference.

I understand that it would be difficult for you to read books with ADHD. Here are some tips for you to carry on with our goal to get better:

- Instead of reading silently, read aloud.

- Take a walk or sprint around the room while reading. This technique may help you to avoid zoning out or focusing on internal distractions rather than the words on the page.

- You can listen to audiobooks or have someone else read to you. This method is particularly useful for persons who learn by listening or who become easily overwhelmed when confronted with a lot of content.

- Choose a hard copy. Researchers have discovered that reading a physical book improves comprehension.

- Take short breaks to move about.

- Discuss what you have just read. Talk to a friend about it, or just think it out loud to yourself.

- Adapt your surroundings. Decide if a quiet reading area or one with some background noise is better for you.

- To avoid losing your place, use a bookmark or a ruler to move down the page as you read each line.

- Consider possible distractions. Is your phone set to silent mode? Is the door shut? Are you hungry? Is it too chilly or too hot for you? Consider and eliminate any potential sources of distraction while reading.

- Keeping a pad of paper handy is a good idea. If internal ideas sidetrack you, scribble them down so you may remember them and return to them later. Set the thought aside for later once you have written it down.

- Personalize the content. Consider how it relates to your own views and personal experiences.

Let's start!

Chapter 1: ADHD Brain Wiring

Do not let anyone make you believe that you are any less capable because you have ADHD. Many of the famous and talented people we find inspiration in, have ADHD!

Andre Brown, a former New York Giants running back, was previously suspended by the NFL (National Football League) after failing a drug test. Brown neglected to mention that he was taking Adderall, a prescribed stimulant, to treat his ADHD.

Jim Carrey is a well-known actor. The actor and comedian is open about his struggles with ADHD and despair.

Solange Knowles is a singer and songwriter. The singer and performer has been diagnosed with ADHD on two occasions. She's become a vocal advocate for a better ADHD diagnosis.

Audra McDonald, a singer, and performer, is the only woman to win six Tony Awards, and she was diagnosed with ADHD.

Michelle Rodriguez is a well-known actress. Because of her ADHD, the Latina actress was expelled from five schools. Rodriguez's career as an actress took off after she discovered it.

Adam Levine, Justin Timberlake, and tons of faces we see today on our screens have ADHD.

So now that we have cleared this point let's understand ADHD better.

1.1 Psychology of ADHD

Attention Deficit Hyperactivity Disorder (formerly known as ADD or Attention Deficit Disorder) is a neurobehavioral illness marked by inattentiveness, distractibility, hyperactivity, and impulsivity as primary symptoms.

ADHD brains are not the same. There are differences in brain anatomy, brain function, and brain development.

- **Brain Function**

    These differences are based on brain size, neurotransmitters, and neural networks. Areas of the ADHD brain may mature more slowly or have differing activity levels than those in a normal brain.

    ADHD has many effects on brain function. Anomalies in behavioral functioning have been linked to the disorder. The modulation of emotions, moods, and brain cell connections can all be affected by ADHD. It can also interrupt message transmission between brain areas.

    Brain connections are made up of neurons, which are clusters of nerve cells that send information throughout the brain. People battling with ADHD may have slower brain networks that are less effective at communicating particular behaviors, messages, or information. These brain networks may operate differently in areas like focus, mobility, and reward.

According to a 2017 research, children with ADHD have somewhat smaller brains than children without ADHD, and their brains may take a lot longer to mature. Size disparities are common in brain regions related to memory, motivation, and emotion regulation, such as the amygdala and hippocampus. It is critical to note that brain size has little to do with intellect.

Children battling with ADHD have delayed brain maturation in specific areas, according to a 2007 publication from the National Institutes of Health. The brain's frontal lobe, which controls attention, cognition, and planning, had the most noticeable delays. In kids with ADHD, the motor cortex was the only brain area that matured faster than usual, explaining symptoms like fidgeting and restlessness.

The frontal lobe is in command of cognitive abilities like impulse control, attention, and social behavior. In patients with ADHD, specific parts of the frontal cortex may mature more slowly. This lag could cause more problems with certain cognitive abilities.

Parts of the frontal lobe related to motor activity and attention capacity are the premotor cortex and prefrontal cortex. In patients with ADHD, these brain parts may be less active.

- **Brain Development**

According to research, some brain regions in children with ADHD are smaller and/or take longer to mature. This is not to say that children with ADHD are not intelligent. It means that areas of their brain develop at a slower rate. These lags occur in the self-management system of the brain. This contains components that aid emotional control as well as a skill known as working memory.

These brain areas tend to be similar in size to those in persons without ADHD by young adulthood. This is not to say that ADHD goes away after adolescence. ADHD symptoms may fluctuate as children get older, but it is a lifetime condition.

Let's get some more clarity on the subject. It will help you understand which of your behavior is due to ADHD.

Symptoms of ADHD

The symptoms listed below are strong indicators that you have ADHD. You are more likely to have ADHD if you have at least seven symptoms and have had them for more than six months.

Symptoms of Inattentiveness:

- Trouble focusing on tasks or even enjoyable activities
- Failure to pay great attention to the smallest details
- When spoken to directly, you frequently do not appear to listen.
- Failure to complete work or comply with instructions
- Having difficulty in staying organized

- Tasks that involve mental effort are difficult for you to do.

- You are prone to misplacing goods that are required for activities.

- Distracted easily

- Distracted day-to-day activities

Inattentive teens likely misplace textbooks or school assignments, forget homework and events, and become easily bored. ADHD could be the cause if you are constantly moaning about how bored you are at school or at other activities, and you seem to forget things all the time.

Symptoms of a Hyperactive/Impulsive Mind:

- Fidget in your seat, tap your hands or feet, or squirm.

- You get out of your seat at inopportune times

- Unable to remain calm or silent

- You talk a lot.

- Frequently give an answer before the question has been fully asked.

- Have a difficult time waiting their turn

- Interrupts or encroaches on the privacy of others

- Have a habit of rushing through assignments and activities.

Hyperactivity and impulsivity have a particularly negative social impact on teenagers. Because your impulsive behavior can be viewed as disrespectful, it is more difficult for you to develop relationships with your peers. Teachers and other authority figures may mistakenly believe that a teen with ADHD is behaving badly when this is not the case.

Now let's do some myth-busting to avoid any confusion.

Myths about ADHD

- **ADHD is not a Medical Condition.** According to science, 1 out of every 4 ADHD patients has a parent who also has the disorder. Furthermore, imaging studies have revealed disparities in brain development between those with ADHD and those who do not.

- **People with ADHD Simply Need to Put in More Effort.** ADHD is not a motivation or laziness issue. Telling someone with ADHD to "just focus" is akin to telling a nearsighted person to "just see farther." Their incapacity to pay attention has nothing to do with their attitude. It is due to differences in how their brains work and how they are structured.

- **With ADHD, you can NEVER Concentrate at any Time.** People with ADHD indeed have a hard time concentrating. However, if they are particularly enthusiastic about something, they may devote all of their attention to it. It is known as hyper focus.

- **ADHD is a type of learning disorder.** Although ADHD symptoms can obstruct learning, they do not create difficulties with specific reading, writing, or math skills. However, several learning difficulties frequently co-occur with ADHD.

Moving on, let's discuss how ADHD affects you in all the good and bad ways.

1.2 Living and Thriving with ADHD

Is ADHD all just about inattention? Let's see what else there is to it.

- **Sleep Problems**

    Sleep disturbances are a side effect of ADHD. It increases your risk of snoring, sleep apnea, and restless legs syndrome (the tendency to move your legs while lying down). It can also cause your body's internal clock, known as the circadian rhythm, to malfunction. As a result, your sleep is out of sync with the sun's natural rising and setting. You may struggle with falling asleep and wake up at regular intervals as a result of this.

- **Impulsive Spending**

    Purchasing items simply because you wish to provide you a short burst of "feel-good" hormones. However, there may be a cost. You can wind up with a depleted bank account or bad credit as a result of your impulsive spending.

- **Missing Deadlines**

    You may get forgetful and distracted if you have ADHD. Because of your focus issues, you are also likely to struggle with time management. Due dates for school, work, and personal commitments may be missed as a result of any of these symptoms.

- **Screen Addiction**

    It is true that ADHD makes it difficult to maintain focus. However, when it comes to cellphones, video games, and televisions, the constant change of images, graphics, comments, and games can captivate your attention. It can be difficult to break yourself away from a screen since your brain craves the reward it receives.

- **Emotional Outbursts**

    One of the ways ADHD affects your brain is that it makes it more difficult for you to manage how you react to situations. You can burst into rage or lash out in frustration or impatience. It could also be the reason you obsess over little details.

- **Relationship Issues**

    When you have ADHD, it is typical for couples to have communication problems, especially if you are not managing your symptoms. It may feel that your partner is always nagging you about certain characteristics of yours, such as forgetfulness or lack of attention.

- **Employment Problems**

    Though every workplace is different, most employers expect you to be organized, attentive, on time, focused, and complete the tasks assigned to you. All of these can be made more difficult by ADHD. As a result, you may not meet your employer's requirements. As a result, keeping a job may be difficult.

- **Chronic Stress**

    Your ADHD symptoms may be causing you stress. When you have this disorder, your stress level is likely to be higher than average for a longer period. Stress can lead to many problems over time, including:

    > Tension and discomfort in the muscles

    > Breathing difficulties

    > Heart problems

    > Having trouble managing your blood sugar levels

    > Problems with digestion

- **Anxiety**

    Anxiety is characterized by persistent worry that prevents you from living your life to your full potential. Anxiety disorders affect almost half of adults with ADHD due to constant anxiety in the early years of life. Your ADHD symptoms can make you feel tense at times. If this is the case, addressing your ADHD will also help you with your anxiety.

- **Compulsive Eating**

    When you have ADHD, you may find it difficult to place limitations on your behavior, e.g., eating. Furthermore, ADHD frequently reduces dopamine levels, a hormone involved in the pleasure area of the brain. Eating is a quick way to boost your dopamine levels and reclaim that happy sensation.

I hope you understand your behavior and habits a bit better now. However, ADHD does not mean your life is doomed, and you cannot do anything about it. There are many traits of ADHD behavior that allow you to accomplish great things. Just Google how many of the great names in the history and present we have fighting with ADHD. ADHD does not have to be a label to keep you from doing things you want to.

Be proud of your attention deficit hyperactivity disorder (ADHD or ADD) and all the creativity, wit, drive, and passion it offers!

- **Hyper Focus**

    Hyper focus, which is a hallmark of ADHD, may be a significant advantage if you can efficiently channel all of that attention and energy into work that matters.

    Many scientists, artists, and writers with ADHD have had highly successful careers, thanks to their capacity to focus on a project for long periods.

- **Creativity**

    While people with this disease are prone to being distracted and inattentive, they also have a tendency to think in a diverse manner. They are able to spot new answers and come up with innovative ideas instead of following fixed methods and patterns of thinking about challenges.

    According to research, persons with ADHD do better in real-time creative activities than people without the disorder.

    According to studies, persons with ADHD see themselves as inherently curious, which they see as a good element of the disorder. Curiosity is an important aspect of creativity. People who are very curious have a strong desire to learn and are receptive to new ideas, which might help them explore new concepts in novel ways.

- **Resilience**

    Living with ADHD comes with its own set of difficulties. Staying focused at work or school, dealing with time management and procrastination, dealing with symptoms that can disrupt social connections, and remembering to take prescriptions are all examples of daily obstacles.

    It takes courage and resilience to face these challenges, which isn't always easy. Resilience is defined as the ability to cope with stress and adversity without resorting to unhealthy coping techniques.

According to one study, most children with ADHD are considered resilient by their parents and instructors.

While setbacks are inevitable, resilience allows persons with ADHD to keep working toward their goals despite obstacles.

- **Conversation Skills and Empathy**

    People with ADHD are frequently excellent communicators. This talent is especially useful for people with ADHD who are more inattentive.

    People with ADHD are frequently talkative, which means they can start a fascinating conversation in almost any situation.

    According to another study, people with ADHD had better levels of social intelligence, emotional recognition, humor, and empathy. Participants in the study acknowledged their own ability to adopt a more positive mental attitude and, as a result, achieve greater "social success."

- **Self-Awareness**

    People with ADHD often develop a greater sense of self-awareness as a result of having to constantly monitor their conduct. Because people with this illness frequently watch their own actions to ensure they are not disrupting others.

The ability to control one's behavior and emotions in response to the demands of the situation is referred to as self-regulation.

While self-regulation is a vital ability, continually monitoring and regulating oneself can lead to mental exhaustion and ego depletion. As a result, people with ADHD may develop coping techniques to assist them in managing their behavior while avoiding exhaustion.

People with ADHD are typically good at analyzing their own feelings and needs and finding strategies to adapt in order to better regulate their behaviors in every given setting as they become more self-aware.

- **Willingness to Take Risks**

    Even when it appeared impossible, Thomas Edison — who may have had ADHD — threw his everything into inventing the light bulb. It took him almost 3,000 tries to produce a working light bulb, but the victory was infinitely sweet because he had to take many risks — and many more failures — to get it to work.

- **Spontaneity**

    Another prevalent characteristic of ADHD is impulsivity. While it is sometimes characterized by rash decisions, impatience, and interrupting others, it can also have advantages. People who can properly manage and channel this symptom can be spontaneous, vibrant, and open to new experiences.

People with ADHD must frequently establish a balance between being overly stimulated and bored. For many people, spontaneous behaviors keep things interesting, resulting in delightful experiences devoid of other distractions.

According to one study, spontaneity has a role in developing courage. Participants in the study frequently regarded themselves as outsiders, and their sense of boldness and adventure were viewed as essential assets.

This spontaneity may aid people in pursuing their hobbies and concentrating on the activities that bring them true delight.

Understanding your own strengths can help you maximize them in a variety of settings and scenarios. For example,

- If you have too much energy, put it to good use by doing something productive. Exercising, for example, can help you burn off surplus energy while also keeping you physically active. You might alternatively put that focus toward achieving other goals at work or school.

- If you have periods where you can use hyper focus, using that time to work on a topic that you are excited about can help you gain new skills and get a lot done.

- Allow yourself the freedom to investigate novel solutions when confronted with a problem. Making art, conversing with a friend, or listening to music, are all examples of activities that might help you to be more creative.

Here's to your thrive drive!

Chapter 2: Focus and Impulsiveness Toolkit

Let's start this chapter with accounts of two ADHD people struggling with focus and impulsivity.

"I am still acutely aware of how my focus wavers, wanders or holds differently than most people of 20 years after my childhood diagnosis of attention deficit hyperactivity disorder (ADHD). I am prone to 'blank' patches in conversations, where I suddenly realize I have no recollection of the previous 30 or so seconds of what has been said, as if someone has skipped through my life's video feed (sometimes, I turn to 'masking,' or fake comprehension - which is embarrassing.) I find it difficult not to fidget and pace when watching television. I detest being the 'owner' of sophisticated paperwork and spreadsheets because I am highly likely to overlook some key element."

"Your mind is racing because you have something to say during a conversation. You are nervous because you need to get that thought out of your head before you forget it. So you cut someone off in the middle of a sentence or finish their notion for them. The conversation has now devolved into a problem.

The lines between what you should say, what you should not, and when to speak up are blurred when you have ADHD. One of the key signs of the disease is impulsive behavior, which can make others angry or hurt and make you feel horrible."

What can we do about it? Let me show you.

2.1 When My Focus is Out of Whack

Living with attention deficit hyperactivity disorder might result in chaotic thoughts and difficulties in concentrating. You may set ambitious goals only to lose focus and abandon them entirely. These 12 tactics are created with ADHD brains in mind. They will help you develop the muscles for true, sustained concentration.

- **Keep in Mind the Zeigarnik Effect**

    The "Zeigarnik Effect" states that unfinished chores are more difficult to get out of your brain than ones that have not been started. Starting a project will make it more difficult for your brain to forget or ignore it, even if you only work on it for 10 minutes. Set a timer for 10 minutes and do something (anything!) during that period if you find yourself daydreaming instead of getting started. The enormous, daunting endeavor will become an unfinished task once you start it, which means your brain will grasp onto it and figure out how to accomplish it.

- **Create a Thought Dump**

When you are trying to pay attention to a task, distractions can be the biggest issues to overcome.

It is tempting to see through each thought that comes to you. You may feel as if these new thoughts and ideas take precedence over what you need to do right now.

When putting everything together for a new TV stand, the thought, "I need to wash my clothes." can disrupt your focus.

You might want to keep a whiteboard or a notepad where you can dump your thoughts to assist you honor the other tasks you wish to finish by staying focused.

As soon as a thought occurs to you, jot it down to be completed later.

- **Eat Right**

Think again if you think your diet has more to do with your weight than your brain. Have you ever come across the term "brain food"? What you eat directly impacts your energy level and capacity to concentrate. Many of your ADHD symptoms, including your inability to concentrate, can be improved by eating a balanced diet. Adults with ADHD should eat protein for breakfast since they will feel sluggish by mid-morning if they only eat carbohydrates, and it is difficult to concentrate when you are fatigued. Limit consuming processed and sugary foods throughout the day. They are quickly digested, creating an increase in blood sugar. Then it drops just as fast, causing ADHD cognitive fog and loss of concentration.

- **Interrupt Yourself**

    Interrupting a task on purpose may assist you in completing it.

    Pulling yourself away from a task, according to experts, increases tension and obsession with the task, which improves your focus. Your brain was focused, then the object of that focus was removed, leaving you feeling unfinished.

    While distractions can be a problem when working on a project, setting the alarm for brief breaks may motivate you to return to what you were doing.

- **Identify Overwhelming Triggers**

    The ADHD brain goes into fight or flight mode when it is agitated. This appears to be a lack of motivation: you binge-watch Netflix instead of doing your laundry or filing your taxes. Identify the triggers that make you feel overwhelmed to break the loop. Hunger is a factor for some, while too many competing priorities are a factor for others. Getting a handle on what causes your overload would not stop it from happening again, but you will be more prepared to recognize it and plan ahead.

- **Make it Exciting**

Make the task more engaging if you are having difficulties concentrating since it is boring. Deal with it the same way you would with a child: if you want him to tidy up his filthy room, have him visualize each item as an airplane, and then he can choose a decent landing site on the shelf for each item. You can use this technique to make job activities more enticing or finish that chore list. You are training yourself how to focus while playing waste basketball with rotten food from the fridge.

- **Use Anchor Words**

    Anchor words or phrases are words or phrases that can help you remember what is important throughout the day. You can help draw your thoughts back to your core aim by repeating particular words or having visual reminders of them.

    For example, repeating or visualizing the word "assignment" can help you get out of a preoccupation. You can also use anchor words to help you refocus throughout a conversation. If you are sitting through a lecture, practicing focusing on specific keywords will help you return your attention to the discussion.

- **Use a Daily Focus List**

    At the start of every day, make a list of your top priorities. This is a terrific approach to blocking out unwanted distractions and refocusing your concentration regularly. A daily focus list consists of a short, bulleted description of three major and three subsidiary goals, which is more than a "to-do list." It is a grounding tool to keep your head out of the clouds and focus on what matters most.

- **Exercise**

    Exercises, like meditation and deep breathing, boost brain function, which is important for ADHD management. To get your heart pounding and your brain in action, incorporate regular exercise into your daily ADHD routine. ADHD patients have a lot of energy. When you exercise, that energy is dissipated, and you can perform better, pay more attention, and focus on what you are doing when you return to work.

- **Go with Your Own Flow**

    Although ADHD comes with a slew of superpowers (such as hyperfocus), you cannot always predict when they'll come into play. Respect your intellect! It is just as crucial to know when you are "in the zone" and able to tackle things that need attention and focus as it is to know when your brain is foggy. Allow yourself to move your attention to less-demanding duties, such as filing paperwork or folding socks, when you are completely out of it. In the long term, you will accomplish more!

- **Give Yourself Notes**

    Notes are useful for reminding you of what you need to concentrate on. They can also be used to motivate others. A message can serve as a gentle reminder to pay your water bill before the end of the day.

Reminding yourself of the project's eventual goal can help you stay motivated. Although installing a deck is challenging, having family and friends over for meals is priceless.

- **Avoid Perfectionism**

    Hyperfocus is not always beneficial. It can sometimes cause people with ADHD to fixate on minor, insignificant matters, sabotaging their actual productivity. Allow yourself to let go of perfectionism and accept "good enough." Do not expect your perfectionist inclinations to vanish overnight — but you may expect to boost your self-esteem, lower your anxiety, and increase your productivity along the road.

- **Prefer Single-Tasking**

    Most of us are multitasking more than ever these days. While this may appear to be a productivity boost, it is actually the contrary. According to research, most people perform poorly at activities while multitasking. Even while single-tasking, people who frequently multitask have a harder time avoiding unnecessary environmental information and switching tasks effectively. According to one study, students who multitasked with computers scored worse in studies, homework, and learning. They also had lower GPAs than kids who normally do only one thing at a time.

    While you would imagine that persons with ADHD are better at multitasking than the typical person, scientific studies show that this is not the case.

    So, for persons with ADHD, one key to focusing is to cease multitasking and make it as easy as possible to focus solely on one task at a time.

- **Take Time to Plan**

    One of the biggest attention drains a lack of planning; it is difficult to stay in the zone when you do not know what you are meant to be doing! It is critical to schedule regular, short planning meetings to sketch out priorities and deadlines for the future days or weeks, as even one minute of preparation can save you up to 40 minutes of labor. Of course, priorities can vary, and emergencies can arise, so nothing is set in stone. Even if you stray off track, having a rough idea of your goals and how to plan to attain them will help you regain your concentration and escape out of La-La Land.

- **Set Deadlines**

    Have you ever wondered why you wait until the last minute to do everything? It is because deadlines are really beneficial to the ADHD brain neurologically: they eliminate conflicting priorities and increase adrenaline, making it easier to go into hyperfocus and focus on a task. However, not every work comes with a clear deadline, so you will have to make your own. These deadlines could be for each part of a project — "I'll get my notes from Lucy on Tuesday at 4 p.m." — or for the entire project: "I need to prepare for my exam by Saturday" Set frequent reminders and visibly display your deadlines to boost your chances of meeting them.

These tricks will help you keep your focus on track and stay in the moment instead of wandering around.

2.2 Where is the Foresight?

It is a classic example of ADHD. You have something to say in the middle of a conversation, but your mind is racing. You are nervous because you need to get that thought out of your head before you forget it. So you cut someone off in the middle of a sentence or finish their thought for them. The discussion has now devolved into a mystery.

The lines between what you should say, what you should not say, and when to speak up, what you should do, and what you should not are blurred when you have ADHD. So here is what you can do to manage this:

- **Understand Your Impulsivity**

    How does your impulsivity show up in your life? What are the most common negative outcomes? When and where do you act the most rashly?

    Taking notes and keeping an inventory will help you become more aware of and recognize the specifics of impulse control issues.

    You will figure out what works best for you with time. To begin, consider the following options:

    - Make a list of recent impulsive behaviors.
    - Outline the negative repercussions of those impulsive activities.
    - Determine the beneficial outcomes of recent impulsive activities

Here's a reminder to STOP:

> **S:** Stop. Get off autopilot mode.

> **T:** Take a slow, deep breath.

> **O:** Observe. Pay attention to how the conversation is progressing, where your attention is focused, your desires, and what's going on in your body.

> **P:** Proceed. Now, either keep going or rectify what is going on in your head and body.

- **Imagine the Future**

Consider the probable ramifications of your actions during the interruptions and delays you cause and if the outcome could be undone. You can get a very good idea of what will happen if you reflect back on your most reckless times in the past. If publicly criticizing your teacher's ideas did not work out the first time, chances are it would not work out this time.

When you have a strong want to say or do something, consider whether it would be beneficial, safe and healthy. Can you think how you can make the outcomes better? Consider how you would feel if you acted on impulse (maybe regretful or ashamed) vs. how you would feel if you acted more thoughtfully and confidently. If it helps, use visual reminders. If you are saving for a vacation but find internet shopping difficult, tape a photo of your holiday destination to your computer so you can see it every time you use it.

- **Keep a Sense of Humor**

You do not have to be so worried about ADHD.

STRATEGY: Learn to say with a smile, "Well, there goes my ADHD talking or acting up again. Sorry for the inconvenience. My mistake. Next time, I'll try to do something about it."

When you say this, you have accomplished four key things:

> You owned your mistake.

> You stated why the mistake happened.

> You apologized and made no excuses by blaming others.

> You mentioned that you would try harder the next time.

I hope these suggestions help you. Moreover, here are a few ways people with ADHD control their impulsive behavior:

- When I am impulsive, I think to myself, "Why do you want that?" Why are you removing all of your things from your desk? Why are you eating so quickly?

- Allowing yourself to indulge sometimes is beneficial. When I don't allow myself any sweets or purchases, I have the most trouble with impulsive behavior. When it comes to blurting things out, cognitive behavioral therapy has taught me to pause, consider the behavior in question, and ask myself, "Is this effective?"

- I can't tell you how many different techniques I've attempted to control my impulsive behavior. I use a combination of approaches: To guarantee that I acquire the products I require; I always go shopping with a written list that includes a maximum spending budget. I utilize self-check questions I developed with a counselor for other impulsive behavior. They include questions like: Is this good for me? Is this something I have the time and ability to do? What impact will this have on my relationships, job, and other critical aspects of my life? Is this something that can be reversed if I decide I don't want it tomorrow?

- I follow a 24-hour rule. This rule gives me time to think about major decisions as an adult with ADHD. I was able to avoid overcommitting my time and resources as a result of this. It has also kept me from sending an enraged email that could have ended a relationship. "That's a fantastic idea," people frequently respond when I tell them I have a 24-hour rule.

- Allowing me to have a different outlet for my urges. For example, instead of interrupting conversations, you could write down your thoughts (on paper or on your phone) or keep an object with you to remind you not to do so. I keep a bottle with me all the time. When your mouth is full of fluids, it is difficult to interrupt, and it also serves as a fidget toy to avoid being distracted.

Try to incorporate these tips into your daily life to maintain focus and avoid impulsivity.

Chapter 3: Organization and Discipline Toolkit

Let's start this chapter with accounts of two ADHD people struggling with organization and discipline.

"My room always looked like it had been bombed, and whenever I tried to straighten it up, I was distracted by books or other things, and I had a bad habit of attempting to clear my floor by stacking things on my bed. It has always been a source of embarrassment for me; I tried my hardest to keep things tidy, but I became overwhelmed and frustrated and could not concentrate."

"Turns out anything I need to get done needs discipline. Hours pass by, and I completely forget that I need to eat. I need to exercise to stay healthy. I need to clean my room more. I need to get my assignments on time. I need to work and find small ways to show up for myself, but I am struggling with getting started."

Let me show you how you can deal with your problems.

3.1 Enough with the Mess

Getting and keeping organized is difficult for people with ADHD. ADHD symptoms such as restlessness, impulsivity, concentrating issues, and other symptoms make it difficult for someone to focus on a boring chore like organizing. When your surroundings and life are disorganized and cluttered, chores are difficult to complete and important things are difficult to find. Everything feels messy and symptoms of ADHD are exacerbated.

It is a vicious cycle. ADHD makes being organized difficult, yet mess exacerbates ADHD symptoms, making organizing even harder. That does not imply that you must give up and just live in misery. Several ADHD organization ideas can help.

- **Set Limit for Decision Making**

    People with ADHD can agonize for days over decisions that others make in seconds. Set a time limit or a budget limit to expedite the procedure. For example, set a deadline for picking a summer camp for your child, and make the best decision you can by that date. If you are looking for a new cell phone, set a budget and avoid the more expensive models.

    Determine the most significant aspect to consider while making a decision: pricing, aesthetics, convenience, practicality, or anything else. When making your decision, concentrate entirely on that factor.

- **Check Your Planner Three Times a Day**

    Organizing ideas can help you better manage your time and activities, whether you have ADHD or simply have too much to remember. Make it a habit to write down all of your upcoming appointments and events on a calendar. Whether it is a day planner, a desk calendar, or a smartphone app makes no difference. It should be kept in one place and checked at least three times a day.

Make it a habit to check your phone at the same time every day.

- **Set Effective Goals**

    It is important to remember that you will need to learn how to set and achieve effective goals. At first glance, goals may not appear to have anything to do with the organization. In reality, however, knowing your goals and how they fit into your life is critical to meeting your organization's expectations.

    When it comes right down to it, anything you try to achieve can be considered a goal. How you organize your resources and time is related to how you organize and achieve your goals. If you do not organize properly, you will not be able to achieve your objectives. In addition, if you fail to set reasonable goals, you will never be able to effectively organize your time and resources to meet your needs. Understanding goals, in the end, is critical to becoming more organized.

    SMART principles should be used to create successful goals. SMART goals are clearly defined and have clear boundaries. They must be precise and quantifiable. This implies that you must have a clear idea of what you want and be able to track your progress. In addition, they must be attainable, reasonable, and time-bound. This implies that you are capable of completing them, that you have reasonable expectations, and that you can see the end in sight.

Daily tasks should ideally be organized around SMART goals. Consider what you want to achieve each day. Then consider whether your goals meet all of the SMART goals. If they do not, you should rethink your expectations. If they do, devise a strategy for achieving all of your objectives.

Keep the number of people to a bare minimum. As you gain experience with SMART goals, you will notice that your overall organizational strategies improve.

- **Fight Hyperfocus**

    Set an alarm clock, a kitchen timer, or a computer alert — or ask a trusted friend or family member to phone you at specific times. You will need this assistance if you are prone to get lost on eBay for hours at a time.

- **Keep Small Items Together**

    Place a small table or bookshelf at your home or room's entryway. On top of it, place a tray or basket to hold vital goods like keys, wallets, glasses, watches, and phones. You can also use this space to keep track of other vital goods like lunchboxes, important papers, and outgoing mail.

- **Keep Your To-Do List Short**

    Regarding ADHD and organizing, keep in mind that persons with ADHD are quickly overwhelmed. Most of the time, an organization fails because you are overwhelmed by everything you have to do.

To get started, you must first simplify the entire process. You cannot see the big picture of everything you have to do. You also would not be able to make and maintain a list of all the tasks.

All that does is remind you of how far you still have to go. To make things easier, to begin with, keep your focus as small as possible and your view as small as possible.

As previously stated, the best course of action is to develop a brief list of a few goals that you wish to achieve each day. You can also write a similar list for your week and month's goals. Make sure to keep each list of objectives to no more than four or five. Then, while you go about completing these tasks, evaluate how well you are doing. Based on your personality, the actual amount may go up or down depending on how you like to do things and how much you can tolerate.

Once you have found a set of goals that works for you, confine your to-do list to that amount of items. Adding any more merely makes the process more complicated and stressful. This does not imply that you are wholly oblivious to or unconcerned about other matters. Rather, you devote your time and energy to the tasks that you are capable of completing. Finally, you will be more organized overall.

- **Use "Wasted" Minutes**

    Make the most of "spare" time. Do not put off organizing tasks until you have a long period of best potential short- and long-term results.

The capability of one's executive function determines one's ability to manage oneself.

Executive functions are the mental processes that allow a person to deliberately and purposefully override instinctual or habitual responses to stimuli and produce a self-determined response in order to achieve short- and long-term goals.

So let me give you some suggestions on it.

- **Start with One Habit**

    I work with many teenagers who let their poor habits get the best of them regularly, and one of the most prevalent issues I see is when they try to alter everything at once. My clients want to practice self-discipline, such as going to bed early, eating on time, and getting things done. This, however, does not work since attempting to cure everything at once is akin to attempting to build Rome in a day. Instead, focus on altering ONE HABIT at a time and on making it easy on yourself. Choose one that you already know how to accomplish but keep putting off.

- **Move Through Yoga**

    Movement can take many different forms. Many of my clients attempt to do yoga six times a week and find it to be one of the most useful exercises they have ever done for managing their ADHD symptoms. It not only relieves tension in your body but also aids in following instructions and maintaining your mind in the current time. Yoga can also help you identify where tension is building up in your body. It permits the 'letting go of tension in each muscle group. It assists us in calming our inner being.

Yoga not only helps you get more movement into your day, but it also helps to stimulate your autonomic nervous system (ANS).

- **Make Tasks Manageable**

    Break down a big assignment or an onerous project that takes several phases and close attention to detail into smaller, more manageable steps that are easier to complete.

    Create a step-by-step plan that keeps you on track from start to end by using a detailed checklist or writing out the individual components of your assignment. It is not necessary to set these actionable items in any particular sequence or even to write them all down at first. You can add items and organize your list in alphabetical or chronological order after you have gotten started and gained some momentum.

    Sometimes you are unsure where to begin, or the scale of the task appears enormous. When you run across these mental or physical stumbling blocks, set a timer and work for brief periods of time.

    Dividing major undertakings into smaller ones is a good idea. Create separate jobs like this instead of one something does not mean never missing a day; it means missing a day, figuring out why, and doing everything you can to avoid it happening again. Start keeping track of your progress if you want to learn how to stick to anything. Try to turn it into a game. How many days can you be consistent with your habits? Set a goal and achieve it, then make these time durations longer.

- **Repeat Actions**

There will come a time when you will not need to keep track of your progress. These habits will become second nature to you. You do not have to think about it or make a decision to do it. There is no justification or opposition. You will just go ahead and do it. This does not imply that you stop giving your full focus to what you are doing or that you stop trying; it simply means that it becomes simpler to do. You develop self-control. The next step is to repeat the process with a new habit.

- **Reward Yourself**

Rewarding yourself for completing a task is a great method to coax your ADHD brain into better habit building and also time management. We think about the repercussions of not doing something all the time. While fear of punishment may work in some cases to motivate us, neuroscience research suggests that incentives may be more motivating than threats of punishment. It is painful to get things done when you are afraid of the repercussions. Why not try it instead if rewards work better and are more enjoyable?

You can use a 45-minute timer on your PC as a trick. You are not allowed to access social media sites while the timer is running. You can use your social media for a few minutes after it is over if you stay on track the entire time.

- **Look for Patterns**

    Figuring out your patterns can help you design your days according to them and maximize productivity. Self-discipline can be strategic and thoughtful. Have you ever noticed how quickly you can recall several instances in which you were unproductive or failed to complete a task or project? It is easy to infer that you are just a slacker who does not get things done. However, you are not giving yourself enough credit. Most people, it turns out, have an easier time remembering moments when they failed than when they succeeded. This is a manifestation of a larger cognitive prejudice known as negativity bias.

    Instead of focusing on instances when you were unproductive, focus on moments when you were in the difficulty zone and working efficiently to combat it. What was the common denominator between these epochs? Was it a particular time of day, a particular work, or a particular subject? When you discover patterns in your peak performance, you will be able to enter those flow states with greater consistency. You can also plan your day to maximize productivity.

- **Eat Healthily**

Bad eating habits do not cause ADHD, but they might take a part in worsening the symptoms. By making modest dietary changes, you might see visible improvements in hyperactivity, distractibility, and stress.

> Throughout the day, eat small meals.

> Sugar and junk food should be avoided as much as possible.

> At each meal, make sure to incorporate a nutritious protein source.

> Each day, aim for several servings of fiber-rich whole grains.

Moreover, certain meals can either improve or aggravate ADHD symptoms. It is critical to pay attention to whether certain meals increase or alleviate your symptoms when dealing with the disease. Proteins, calcium, fatty acids, vitamin B, and magnesium aid in properly fueling your body and brain and may help to alleviate ADHD symptoms.

Some meals and food additives have been linked to some people's aggravation of ADHD symptoms. Foods high in sugar and fat, for example, may be recommended to avoid. Certain additives that improve the flavor, taste, and appearance of foods, such as MSG, sodium benzoate (a preservative), and red and yellow colors, may increase ADHD symptoms. Artificial colors and sodium benzoate were connected to increased hyperactivity in children of various ages, regardless of whether or not they had ADHD, according to a 2007 study.

- **Write it Down**

    It has been proved that writing down your thoughts and emotions might help you relax. If you are dealing with stress on a regular basis, keep a diary and scribble down the events or activities that make you worried; it may seem like a simple remedy, but having to write everything down will force you to acknowledge and actively handle your stressors.

- **Take Time to Play**

    You set yourself up for burnout by not taking pauses from today's hectic lifestyle. Make time for fun in your life. Every week, have supper or go to the movies with pals. On the weekend, go for a drive across the countryside or to the beach. Find out what you enjoy doing and go for it without feeling guilty.

- **Avoid Overstimulation**

    Many persons with ADHD suffer from bouts of overstimulation, in which they are overwhelmed by a barrage of stimuli. ADHD symptoms may be triggered in crowded places like music halls and amusement parks. Allowing enough personal space is vital for averting outbursts; thus, staying away from crowded restaurants, busy supermarkets, rush hour traffic, and high-traffic malls may help alleviate ADHD symptoms.

- **Create Boundaries**

    Overbooking your schedule can cause you to become stressed. Stress takes its toll on your thinking, whether the cause is sheer impulsivity or an internal voice suggesting, "I should do x, y, z." Three times a day, practice saying no. And ask yourself, "What am I saying 'no' to?" every time you say "yes." Listening to music? Relaxation?

- **Limit Technology Use**

    Computers, television, cell phones, and the Internet all provide constant electronic stimulation, which can exacerbate symptoms. Although there is a great discussion regarding whether viewing television has an impact on ADHD, it may exacerbate symptoms. ADHD is not caused by flashing pictures or excessive noise. However, a glaring screen exacerbates the problem if you are having trouble concentrating.

    Make it a point to keep track of how much time you spend on the web and watching television and to limit your viewing to specific times.

- **Measure Time**

    Time is a fluid concept for most persons with ADHD. Buy a beeping wristwatch and set it to go off every hour to help you keep track of time. Get a countdown timer that will sound after five minutes if you always require "just five more minutes."

You can spend hours on the Internet and then find yourself scurrying to fulfill deadlines at the end of the day. A stopwatch, programmed to go off every hour, can shake you out of your online trance.

- **Keep a Positive Attitude**

    Even if you feel stressed, attempt to counteract it by thinking happy thoughts and directing your energy toward things you enjoy, but keep in mind that there are limits to this. Allow yourself to take a break every now and then to do something you enjoy, such as spending time outside, relaxing with a good book, or socializing with friends and family. Remember, having stress as a result of, or in addition to, your ADHD is entirely normal, and it is alright not to be okay occasionally.

I hope these strategies will help you keep your stress in check. Let's move on to tips for anxiety control.

4.2 Ease Up the Anxiety

Anxiety symptoms are more intense in people with ADHD and anxiety problems than in people who do not have ADHD. However, even individuals with ADHD who do not fit the diagnostic criteria for anxiety may suffer occasional and situational worry in their daily lives – because ADHD can create time blindness, impaired working memory, and amplified emotions, among other things anxiety-inducing symptoms.

Researchers found that difficulties associated with ADHD, such as procrastination, tardiness, and the threat of social stigma, all caused individuals to experience anxiety at various periods throughout their life, and once they were stressed, their ADHD symptoms worsened.

Here is what you can do about this problem:

- **Regulate Emotions, Mindset, and Behavior**

    Start by using your sensations and behaviors as knowledge to properly control your anxiety. Anxiety or any troublesome feeling can prompt you to think. A good follow-up inquiry includes:

    ➢ What is this discomfort trying to tell me?

    ➢ What am I feeling?

    ➢ What exactly is the issue?

    ➢ What was the driving factor?

    ➢ Is the issue truly a problem? If that is the case, how can it be dealt with?

    ➢ What is the issue's best, worst, and most likely outcome?

    Using writing, continue this disentanglement practice. Making notes on your computer or phone is good, but writing out tensions and worries with a pen and paper is more therapeutic and engaging. In either case, getting the issue out of your head and seeing it as text can help you realize what you have control over and what you do not. Exposure — coming face to face with the problem – is also a part of the activity.

Here is an example of the exercise in action: Let's say you find yourself self-medicating with binge eating. How do you deal with these compulsions?

"How am I feeling?" you might wonder. What is the advantage of this type of behavior? "Why am I going to get out of this?" These actions are frequently linked to anxiety reduction, stress numbing, and a sense of control. Labeling the emotion (anxiety, overload, or loss of control) is also a way of acknowledging the circumstance, which is a calming action.

Determine the issues or causes that led to the bingeing or self-medicating behavior. Boredom, loneliness, anxieties about meeting obligations, unrest or conflict at home, work-related stress, and even the news cycle are all examples.

Consider these issues and triggers carefully. Are the issues listed really issues? Perhaps you set an unrealistic deadline for yourself to meet the commitment you are worried about. What are the best and worst-case situations and the most likely outcomes? Thinking about these things can help us focus on the probabilities rather than the possibilities — the problem might not be a problem at all.

However, self-medicating with bingeing are issues that must be addressed. Suppression control – removing temptations from home – and replacement behaviors, such as swapping in healthy meals, finding stimulation in tea, or listening to calming music, are two ways to deal with it.

- **Make Use of Smartphone Apps**

    Numerous apps available can assist us in finding peace at the moment, help fall asleep, or provide a playlist that we can access if we are experiencing anxiety. I meditate on my phone, utilizing Insight Timer as my go-to app. When you buy a yearly subscription, you can listen offline, which saves data and reduces the number of radio waves broadcast at night. I mostly use it for meditation at night and for a body scan meditation during the day.

    If I listen to music on an app like Spotify, I have multiple playlists set up for different purposes. I will listen to one of my incredibly relaxing playlists if I need to relax. Set things up ahead of time to make them easier to find when you need them.

- **Find Quiet Places**

    Finding a quiet spot these days can be difficult, but all we have to do is to use our thinking brain to find something that works for us. At the moment, my peaceful area is a relatively private beach near my home. Try a park or a garden, which may or may not be accessible to everyone. Being in the presence of trees appears to have a calming impact.

Being close to nature makes it easier to reset and refocus, especially when there is less external noise and stimulation. Look for the still place within yourself. It is right there. It is a lot easier if you practice.

Put a "do not disturb" sign on your door if you are inside a house or apartment so you can enjoy some alone time. Disrupting from our immediate environment aids in discovering a still point within oneself, which leads to an improved feeling of calmness. This is not anything you will come up with overnight. It takes time and effort to master.

- **Specify Tasks**

Fill your calendar with time or task-based items instead of broadly-defined activities. Checking emails can be a 5-emails or 5-minute effort, and reviewing an essay can be a 15-minute or 15-page task. Clearly, laying out activities combats front-end perfectionism and makes it simple to engage in an activity that you are not "in the mood" for. Discomfort disappears quickly after engagement.

- **Stay Grounded**

When we are stressed, we are more likely to have negative thoughts. We are concerned about the future and ruminate on past negative events. You can avoid being swept away by negative thoughts by anchoring yourself in the current moment.

Focus on your five senses and pay attention to the environment around you the next time you find yourself thinking about the past or future. Use a grounding practice or guided meditation to help you relax. Start a daily mindfulness practice to prevent unpleasant thoughts and emotions from spiraling out of control in the future.

- **Find and Use Your Creativity**

   I believe that everyone has the ability to be creative but most of us lack time to discover our inner creative genius. Drawing, writing, painting, or doing anything with our hands seems to be a great method to express ourselves or let go of pent-up feelings. Use an iPad and a stylus if you do not want to write on paper. If you want to color but do not want to do the work, many applications are available that feature coloring or design programs.

- **Master a Skill**

   This method is ideal for ADHD teens who suffer from depression or a sense of powerlessness. You boost your self-esteem and sense of self-worth when you spend time doing things you enjoy.

   Doing what you enjoy can make you happier and more resilient. You will be able to handle setbacks more easily if you have more "mastery moments."

- **Try Meditation**

    Meditation and guided imagery are available in a variety of forms. Imagine yourself in a serene or relaxing environment for guided imagery. The location could be genuine or imagined. Focus on exploring this tranquil or relaxing location with your five senses, fully immersing yourself in the experience and envisioning yourself in that atmosphere. If this seems too hard, some people find it more beneficial to simply let disturbing thoughts pass through their minds. Imagine yourself lying by a stream as one way to achieve this. Imagine a thought entering your mind and immediately leaving it, carried away by the flowing water.

- **Connect with Nature**

    Being inside might sometimes make you feel more worried, especially if there is clutter or a lot of stuff around you. Wide-open areas, such as beaches or parks, might help you relax significantly.

    If you have never heard of 'grounding' or 'earthing,' which involves placing your bare feet on the ground, you are in for a treat. Connecting with the ground has been shown to have a soothing effect on the body and reduce inflammation and treat inflammatory illnesses. Is not that the simplest form of treatment you can think of? What is more, it is completely free!

Earthing or grounding may sound strange or far-fetched, yet it works by reuniting our bodies with the earth.

There is something about attaching our bare feet to the ground, whether we are grounding or earthing ourselves at the beach or just out in the yard, that helps us release energy. It is also known to aid in sleep, which is something that everyone with ADHD could use more of! - Take off your shoes. Place your feet on the ground. Feel the difference.

- **Practice Deep Breathing**

When you are anxious, your symptoms can become magnified, leading to a cascade of negative consequences: inconsistent sleep, chronic exhaustion, dietary issues, weight gain, cardiac disease, and hypertension can all occur or worsen as a result of stress and anxiety. Here are a few exercises of deep breathing through which you can manage anxiety:

> **Box Breathing**

Box breathing, also known as four-square breathing, is a simple technique to learn and master. This form of paced breathing is already known to you if you have ever caught yourself inhaling and exhaling to the beat of music. This is how it goes:

o To a count of four, exhale.

- Hold your breath for four counts with your lungs empty.
- Inhale for four counts.
- For a count of four, hold your breath in your lungs.
- Exhale and repeat the cycle.

➤ **Belly Breathing**

The American Institute of Stress recommends 20 to 30 minutes of "belly breathing" daily to alleviate stress and anxiety.

- Find a quiet, comfortable spot to sit or lie down. All good options include sitting on a chair, sitting cross-legged, or reclining on your back with a small cushion under your knees and another under your head.
- Place one hand on your stomach, just below your ribs, and the other on your upper chest.
- Allow your stomach to relax without tightening or clenching your muscles to push it inward.
- Slowly inhale through your nose. The air should go into your nose and down, allowing your stomach to rise with one hand and collapse inward with the other (toward your spine).

- Slowly exhale with slightly pursed lips. Keep an eye on the hand on your chest, which should be fairly still.

- Although the sequence frequency will vary depending on your health, most people start with three repetitions and gradually increase from five to ten minutes, one to four times each day.

➤ **Resonance Breathing**

Coherent breathing, also known as resonance breathing, might help you relax and reduce anxiety.

- Close your eyes and lie down.

- Breathe in slowly via your nose, mouth closed, for six seconds. Do not fill your lungs with air too much.

- Allow your breath to gently leave your body for six seconds without straining it.

- Continue for a total of ten minutes.

- Spend a few more minutes being still and concentrating on how your body feels.

These techniques will help you manage your anxiety and stress. ADHD cannot stop you from doing anything you want!

Conclusion

For anyone, adolescence may be a trying time. Adolescents with attention deficit hyperactivity disorder (ADHD) experience additional pressures and problems.

Though many people associate ADHD with children, symptoms can persist throughout adolescence and adulthood. A teen dealing with all of the other changes that come with puberty and growing independence also has to deal with the additional challenge of having ADHD.

The world can be a maddening swirl for a teen with ADHD. Routine duties such as planning ahead, accomplishing work, staying on track, scheduling activities, and following conversations can be stressful. Obstacles sometimes appear to be insurmountable. Restlessness is a common symptom of ADHD in teenagers.

These symptoms can have an impact on a teen's life in a variety of ways. It can affect their social, academic, and personal lives.

The inspiration behind "Managing ADHD at Young Age for Teens" is to help teens survive and thrive with this disorder. The book includes four chapters, with the first one devoted to building an understanding of ADHD.

Chapter one starts by explaining the psychology of ADHD and its effects on brain structure, function, and development. Moving on, it identifies the symptoms of ADHD and busts popular myths associated with it. Lastly, it discusses the downsides and upsides of ADHD to help teens understand themselves better.

The rest of the book focuses on strategies to deal with the most common issues of ADHD. The second chapter deals with maintaining focus and avoiding impulsivity. The former issue includes tips like keeping the Zeigarnik Effect in mind, creating a thought dump, interrupting yourself, identifying overwhelming triggers, making it exciting, etc. The latter issue includes tips like understanding your impulsivity, being mindful, stopping the action, removing triggers, staying present, imagining the future, etc.

The third chapter is dedicated to organization and discipline. It includes strategies for organization such as setting a limit for decision making, checking your planner three times a day, setting effective goals, fighting hyperfocus, keeping small items together, using "Wasted" Minutes, simplifying your wardrobe, etc. It includes strategies for a discipline such as starting with one habit, moving through yoga, making tasks manageable, committing to just starting, sticking to your habits, looking for patterns, etc.

The fourth chapter discusses stress and anxiety. It includes strategies for stress such as making structure your friend, slowing down, eating healthily, writing it down, taking time to play, avoiding overstimulation, creating boundaries, limiting technology use, etc. later, it includes strategies for anxiety such as regulating emotions, mindset, and behavior, making use of smartphone apps, specifying tasks, staying grounded, mastering a skill, finding and using your creativity, etc.

I have developed this book with my extensive knowledge and experience of ADHD as a behavioral therapist. If this book was helpful to you, please leave a review on Amazon!

Printed in Great Britain
by Amazon